JOKE BOOK

TRY NOT TO LAUGH

7 YEAR OLD EDITION

CHALLENGE™

Try Not To Laugh Challenge
BONUS PLAY

Join our Joke Club and get the Bonus Play PDF!

Simply send us an email to:

TNTLPublishing@gmail.com

and you will get the following:

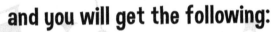

- 10 Hilarious, Bonus Jokes
- An entry in our Monthly Giveaway of a $50 Amazon Gift card!

We draw a new winner each month and will contact you via email!

Good luck!

WELCOME TO THE
TRY NOT TO LAUGH CHALLENGE!

RULES OF THE GAME:

★ Grab a friend or family member, a pen/pencil, and your comedic skills! Determine who will be "Jokester 1" and "Jokester 2".

★ Take turns reading the jokes aloud to each other, and check the box next to each joke you get a laugh from! Each laugh box is worth 1 point, and the pages are labeled to instruct and guide when it is each player's turn.

★ Once you have both completed telling jokes in the round, tally up your laugh points and mark it down on each score page! There is a total of 10 Rounds.

★ Play as many rounds as you like! Once you reach the last round, Round 10, tally up ALL points from the previous rounds to determine who is the CHAMPION LAUGH MASTER!

★ Round 11 - The Tie-Breaker Round.

In the event of a tie, proceed to Round 11. This round will be 'Winner Takes All!', so whoever scores more laugh points in this round alone, is crowned the CHAMPION LAUGH MASTER!

TIP: Use an expressive voice, facial expressions, and even silly body movement to really get the most out of each joke and keep the crowd laughing!

Now, it's time to play!

ROUND

1

What is an Android's favorite dance move?

The Robot.

☐ LAUGH

What do you call a superhero you can't eat?

The In-EDIBLE Hulk!

☐ LAUGH

What do you say to two doors that are fighting?

"KNOCK it off!"

☐ LAUGH

Where do you go to put fuel in your horse?

The Grass Station.

☐ LAUGH

Why are vowels so good at baseball?

They always keep their "I" on the ball!

○ LAUGH

Why did no one trust the cell phone?

It was acting PHONE-y.

○ LAUGH

What do vampire's do when they get together?

Go get a bite to eat.

○ LAUGH

What do you find in the dinosaur junkyard?

T-WRECKS! (T-Rex)

○ LAUGH

Pass the book to Jokester 2! →

Where do stylish ghosts shop?

At a BOO-tique!

○ LAUGH

What kind of bird installs doorbells?

A buzzard.

○ LAUGH

What was the leopard's favorite app?

SPOT-ify!

○ LAUGH

Why did the pirate get detention?

He played HOOK-y!

○ LAUGH

Why did the cardigan smell so bad?

He was a real SWEAT-er.

LAUGH

What do digital watches like to drink at lunch?

CLOCK-olate Milk!

LAUGH

What did Mr. Freeze say to his angry friend?

"CHILL out!"

LAUGH

What do you call it when the sun is in a good mood?

Sunny delight!

LAUGH

Time to add up your points! →

SCORE BOARD

Add up each Jokester's laugh points for this round!

 **JOKESTER 1** $\dfrac{}{\text{Total}}$ /8

 **JOKESTER 2** $\dfrac{}{\text{Total}}$ /8

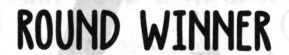

ROUND WINNER

ROUND

2

 **JOKESTER 1**

Why was the snake embarrassed?

He was sss-NAKED!

⬜ LAUGH

What do you call it when your bike tire is flat?

A wheel problem.

⬜ LAUGH

What do farm animals eat for breakfast?

GOAT-meal.

⬜ LAUGH

What do you tell a dog that won't sit still?

"Paws!" (Pause)

⬜ LAUGH

Why is the freezer so mean?

It's always cold!

☐ LAUGH

Why do trees make great cheerleaders?

They're always ROOTING for you!

☐ LAUGH

What did the beach say, when the water asked him to help him move?

"Shore!" (Sure)

☐ LAUGH

How do you reject someone from Neverland?

"Get Lost, Boy."

☐ LAUGH

Pass the book to Jokester 2! ➜

Why are flamingos always so happy?

They've been tickled pink! ☐ LAUGH

Do you know what an owl would say if it could speak?

"I haven't got a HOO!" ☐ LAUGH

What do horses do when they're out of butter?

They ask their NEIGHHH-bor! ☐ LAUGH

Why did the lion go to the repair shop?

For some MANE-tenance! ☐ LAUGH

What did the snowman say once he had solved the riddle?

"That was a sNOw-brainer!"

LAUGH

When does spaghetti get dressed up?

When it wants to look good for the meat-BALL!

LAUGH

How do letters gamble?

They place alpha-BETS.

LAUGH

What did the shirt say to the noisy pants?

"Zip it!"

LAUGH

Time to add up your points! →

SCORE BOARD

Add up each Jokester's laugh points for this round!

JOKESTER 1

$$\frac{\qquad}{\text{Total}} \, /8$$

JOKESTER 2

$$\frac{\qquad}{\text{Total}} \, /8$$

$$\frac{\qquad}{}$$

ROUND WINNER

ROUND
3

What superhero group likes to show off their muscles?

The FLEX-Men! (X-Men)

LAUGH

What's a dinosaur's favorite video game console?

A REX-Box!

LAUGH

What kind of toy car likes to make people angry online?

Remote con-TROLL-ed cars!

LAUGH

What do you call giant robots who work on a ranch?

Trans-FARMERS! (Transformers)

LAUGH

Why is the pencil always correct?

He's always WRITE.

☐ LAUGH

What did the cat say after getting a splinter?

"Me-OWW!"

☐ LAUGH

What insect is most easily scared?

A flea!

☐ LAUGH

Why did the man gain weight in his sleep?

He had too many sweet dreams!

☐ LAUGH

Pass the book to Jokester 2! ➔

How easy is it to eat a circular confection?

It's a piece of cake!

LAUGH

What type of blankets do armadillos love?

Quilts!

LAUGH

How do you solve a mystery on the ocean floor?

You get to the bottom of it!

LAUGH

What do you get when you cross an iPod with a fridge?

Cool music.

LAUGH

Why do dogs always smile?

They're so PAWS-itive!

☐ LAUGH

What's a shark's favorite tool?

It's either a HAMMER-head or a SAW-fish!

 ☐ LAUGH

What happened to the chip that fell into the sofa cushions?

It became a couch potato.

 ☐ LAUGH

Why are people who study reptiles also great musicians?

They know all the SCALES!

 ☐ LAUGH

Time to add up your points! ➜

SCORE BOARD

Add up each Jokester's laugh points
for this round!

JOKESTER 1

$\dfrac{/8}{\text{Total}}$

JOKESTER 2

$\dfrac{/8}{\text{Total}}$

ROUND WINNER

ROUND

4

Why was the ice cube afraid?

It was in hot water!

LAUGH

What kind of snack is a computer's favorite?

Chips!

LAUGH

Who is the sweetest Looney Tunes character?

TAFFY Duck!

LAUGH

What treat were the silent children given?

Shhh-gar!

LAUGH

What does a walrus use to write?

A PEN-guin.

☐ LAUGH

What do you call pork that knows martial arts?

A Karate Pork CHOP!

☐ LAUGH

What do you call a circus for lions?

'The Mane Event.'

☐ LAUGH

What do crayfish draw with?

CRAY-ons.

☐ LAUGH

Pass the book to Jokester 2! →

What kind of communication device does a genius use?

A smartphone.

☐ LAUGH

What did the hammer say after completing the job?

"Nailed it!"

☐ LAUGH

What do you call a contest for the muddiest river?

A SWAMP-etition!

☐ LAUGH

What's a cat's favorite pizza topping?

Pep-PURR-roni!

☐ LAUGH

Which moon tastes the best?

A HONEY-moon.

⬭ LAUGH

Which state in America asks the most questions?

WHY-oming.

⬭ LAUGH

What kind of art do dentists like?

PAIN-tings!

⬭ LAUGH

Why did the boxer fight the piano?

He wanted to hit the right note!

⬭ LAUGH

Time to add up your points! ➝

SCORE BOARD

Add up each Jokester's laugh points
for this round!

JOKESTER 1

$\dfrac{}{\text{Total}}$ /8

JOKESTER 2

$\dfrac{}{\text{Total}}$ /8

ROUND WINNER

ROUND

5

What's a hound dog's favorite sport?

BASSET-ball.

☐ LAUGH

My cat is never serious. He's always KITTEN around!

☐ LAUGH

Why does the spider love ducks?

They have WEB-bed feet.

☐ LAUGH

What do chickens like to do on a rainy day?

Read a BAWK!

☐ LAUGH

Which creatures make sure the ocean is clean underwater?

Mer-MAIDS and Mer-BUTLERS!

LAUGH

What insect loves margarine?

BUTTER-flies!

○
LAUGH

What's the best way to drink your fruit juice?

Through a STRAW-berry!

○
LAUGH

Why did the hamburgers go ice-skating?

They were sliders!

LAUGH

Pass the book to Jokester 2! →

How did the king congratulate his best soldier?

He said, "Good Knight!"

☐ LAUGH

Why does an astronaut wear a full-body suit?

So their pants don't fall down and MOON people!

☐ LAUGH

What trees are the warmest to be around?

FIR trees.

☐ LAUGH

What do you call ice cream on two wheels?

Bi-cicles.

☐ LAUGH

What farm animals are the comfiest?

Pigs in a blanket!

LAUGH

What's the nosiest turtle?

A Snapping Turtle.

LAUGH

What's a piece of furniture's favorite food?

A CHAIR-y! (Cherry)

LAUGH

What kind of dog loves to eat?

A Chow Chow.

LAUGH

Time to add up your points! →

SCORE BOARD

Add up each Jokester's laugh points for this round!

JOKESTER 1

/8
Total

JOKESTER 2

/8
Total

ROUND WINNER

ROUND

6

 **JOKESTER 1**

Why is pizza from Mars so good?

Because it's out of this world!   ☐ LAUGH

Where do they hold food competitions?

At Stadi-YUMS!   ☐ LAUGH

If people ride bicycles, what do snowmen ride?

Icicles.   ☐ LAUGH

What is the librarian's favorite animal?

Shhhhhheep.   ☐ LAUGH

How did the owl win the competition?

With its great TALON-ts!

LAUGH

What happened to the singer who performed for ghosts?

They got BOO-ed off stage!

LAUGH

What do you call a cherry on a spinning toy?

The cherry on top!

LAUGH

Why was the baker running?

The recipe asked for a DASH of salt.

LAUGH

Pass the book to Jokester 2! ➝

What happens to a banana with a sunburn?

It starts to PEEL.

☐ LAUGH

What's your favorite kind of pizza?

The kind I get to eat.

☐ LAUGH

What did the alligator put on his kitchen floor?

Rep-TILES.

☐ LAUGH

Did you hear that the 3 little pigs opened a spa?

I hear the mud baths are great!

☐ LAUGH

What is a banana split's favorite day of the week?

Sundae!

☐ LAUGH

How do Hot Pockets give a warm hello?

With a micro-WAVE!

☐ LAUGH

What is the soup's favorite way to relax?

Going BOWL-ing!

☐ LAUGH

What kind of dessert do you eat at a parade?

An Ice-Cream Float!

☐ LAUGH

Time to add up your points! →

SCORE BOARD

Add up each Jokester's laugh points
for this round!

JOKESTER 1

$\dfrac{\quad /8\quad}{\text{Total}}$

JOKESTER 2
$\dfrac{\quad /8\quad}{\text{Total}}$

ROUND WINNER

ROUND

7

What do drummers eat?

Drum ROLLS!

 LAUGH

Why did the goat eat a light bulb?

He just wanted a LIGHT lunch!

 LAUGH

What do spring clouds say when asked about the weather?

"I don't snow!"

 LAUGH

How does the ocean say 'goodbye'?

"SEA you later!"

 LAUGH

What bug likes to eat?

A MEAL-worm.

 LAUGH

What kind of art do fish like?

Watercolor.

LAUGH

How do cats gossip?

They Whisker! (Whisper)

LAUGH

What is a pig's favorite tool?

HAM-mers!

 LAUGH

Pass the book to Jokester 2! →

What did the man say, when he learned the whole country turned into cars?

"What in CAR-nation?!"

LAUGH

Why did the tennis player's neighbor not like them?

They kept raising a RACKET!

LAUGH

What's a square's favorite board game?

Connect Four!

LAUGH

Where do galoshes send their children in the summer?

BOOT Camp!

LAUGH

What do you call it when you throw and catch dogs in the air?

PUG-gling! (Juggling)

◯ LAUGH

What's the opposite of no land?

Is-land!

◯ LAUGH

Why were all the fish so impressed?

They were in SHARK and awe!

◯ LAUGH

What two letters can you find in liquid form?

T and P.

◯ LAUGH

Time to add up your points! →

SCORE BOARD

Add up each Jokester's laugh points for this round!

JOKESTER 1
$$\frac{\qquad}{\text{Total}} 18$$

JOKESTER 2
$$\frac{\qquad}{\text{Total}} 18$$

ROUND WINNER

ROUND

8

 **JOKESTER 1**

The nachos tried telling jokes, but they were way too cheesy!

☐ LAUGH

What did the jelly say to the peanut butter?

"Stick with me, kid."

☐ LAUGH

What kind of seafood can you find at the North Pole?

Frozen fish!

☐ LAUGH

What do indifferent vegetables say?

"I do not CARROT-all."

☐ LAUGH

What card game do you find at an underwater traffic light?

Go Fish!

◻ LAUGH

What do you call Mr. Potato Head after he works out?

'A Spud Stud.'

◻ LAUGH

Why was Humpty Dumpty upset when it started snowing in winter?

Because he had a great FALL!

◻ LAUGH

What's orange and flat?

An orange that got run over!

◻ LAUGH

Pass the book to Jokester 2! →

What is a hornet's favorite coat?

His Yellowjacket!

☐ LAUGH

What do you call a cat that doesn't play fair?

A CHEAT-ah!

☐ LAUGH

What is a shark's favorite meal?

School lunch!

☐ LAUGH

How do crabs wash dishes?

With a Sea Sponge.

☐ LAUGH

What's a rapper's favorite toy?

A YO-YO!

☐ LAUGH

What kind of knees are on top of a house?

Chim-KNEES!

☐ LAUGH

What do you call cups that see really well?

Glasses!

☐ LAUGH

Why is the wind always happy?

Because life is a breeze!

☐ LAUGH

Time to add up your points! →

SCORE BOARD

Add up each Jokester's laugh points
for this round!

JOKESTER 1

/8
_____
Total

JOKESTER 2

/8
_____
Total

_____
ROUND WINNER

ROUND

9

How do fish do their research?

The Inter-NET!

LAUGH

Why did the dog need a nap?

It had a RUFF day!

LAUGH

What do you call an alligator who hangs out on dark streets?

An ALLEY-gator!

LAUGH

At the Halloween party, why did the kids run away?

The MUMMY arrived!

LAUGH

JOKESTER 1

Which mammals hit the most home runs?

Bats!

LAUGH

Why did the ghost have a stuffy nose?

To many BOO-gers!

LAUGH

What did the cat do when he got ambushed by bugs?

He decided to FLEA!

LAUGH

How do hermit crabs stay safe?

They're always looking for SHELL-ter!

LAUGH

Pass the book to Jokester 2! →

What do you call it when you cross a flower and a cat?

A Dandy-LION!

☐ LAUGH

Who always wins first place in the ocean?

The GOLD-fish!

☐ LAUGH

What does a pig use on his cuts?

OINK-ment!

☐ LAUGH

Why don't whales have jobs?

They just wanna have fin! (Fun)

☐ LAUGH

What did the burrito say to the sad salsa?

"Do you want to TACO about it?" ☐ LAUGH

What type of music does corn listen to?

POP Music. ☐ LAUGH

What type of shoes do bananas wear?

Slippers. ☐ LAUGH

What do you call an entertaining onion?

☐ LAUGH

A Funyun!

Time to add up your points! →

SCORE BOARD

Add up each Jokester's laugh points for this round!

JOKESTER 1

$\dfrac{/8}{\text{Total}}$

JOKESTER 2

$\dfrac{/8}{\text{Total}}$

ROUND WINNER

ROUND

10

 **JOKESTER 1**

Which superhero can't be out during the full moon?

Were-WOLVERINE!

 LAUGH

What board game has grumpy hippopotamuses?

'Hangry Hangry Hippos!'

 LAUGH

What do you call a flying insect who is too heavy?

A draggin' fly! (Dragonfly)

 LAUGH

What basketball team did the hip-hop artist like to root for?

The Toronto RAP-tors!

 LAUGH

Why did the potato put sunscreen on at the beach?

It was always getting french fried! ☐ LAUGH

What kind of glasses do turkeys drink from?

Gobble-ts! ☐ LAUGH

Why did the bungee jumper go shopping?

She needed a FALL wardrobe! ☐ LAUGH

What wild animal should you never play Monopoly with?

A cheetah! ☐ LAUGH

Pass the book to Jokester 2! →

Why was the sponge a good student?

It knew how to SOAK everything in!

⬜ LAUGH

Why did the octopus love camping?

It had TENT-acles!

⬜ LAUGH

What do you call a tumbling class coach?

A ROLL model.

⬜ LAUGH

What do you call it when guitars go crazy?

Looney Tunes!

⬜ LAUGH

Why was the rabbit cranky?

He was having a bad HARE day.

◯ LAUGH

Why are pigs always so happy?

Because nothing BOARS them!

◯ LAUGH

Why does Netflix have so many fish?

It's always streaming!

◯ LAUGH

What do you call numerous ponies on a stage?

Horse Play.

◯ LAUGH

Time to add up your points! →

67

SCORE BOARD

Add up each Jokester's laugh points
for this round!

JOKESTER 1
$$\frac{\qquad}{\text{Total}} /8$$

JOKESTER 2
$$\frac{\qquad}{\text{Total}} /8$$

$$\frac{\qquad\qquad\qquad\qquad}{\text{ROUND WINNER}}$$

Add up all your points from each round.
The Jokester with the most points is crowned

The Laugh Master!

In the event of a tie, continue to Round 11
- The Tie-Breaker Round!

JOKESTER 1

—————
Grand Total

JOKESTER 2

—————
Grand Total

THE LAUGH MASTER

ROUND
11

TIE-BREAKER
(Winner Takes ALL!)

I always thought that tadpoles were a little fishy...

☐ LAUGH

What did the chicken say when asked, "How are you doing"?

"I'm doing EGG-cellent!"

☐ LAUGH

Why did the ponies get in trouble?

They wouldn't stop horsing around!

☐ LAUGH

Which bug has 9 lives?

A CAT-erpillar!

☐ LAUGH

 **JOKESTER 1**

What kind of horse doesn't like hay?

A Seahorse.

○ LAUGH

How did the apple bruise the banana?

With a fruit PUNCH!

○ LAUGH

What kind of hot sauce makes food colder?

Chilly sauce!

○ LAUGH

What did the egg say to his funny spatula friend?

"You crack me up!"

○ LAUGH

Pass the book to Jokester 2! →

Fruit is Vegetable's best friend. After all, they do make a great PEAR!

LAUGH

Which stone tastes sour?

LIME-stone.

LAUGH

Why should you knit socks for your soulmate?

To show that you're THREAD over heels!

LAUGH

What color should the flag for a public library be?

A READ flag!

LAUGH

What game do you play when someone is at your door?

Guess Who!

○ LAUGH

Why are football players good at fishing?

They all have their TACKLE boxes!

○ LAUGH

Why did the first baseman buy a treadmill?

So he could get more home runs!

○ LAUGH

At first, the fish was giving me trouble, but I let him off the hook.

○ LAUGH

Time to add up your points! →

Add up all your points from the
Tie-Breaker Round.
The Jokester with the most points is crowned

The Laugh Master!

JOKESTER 1   /8
                   _____
                    Total

JOKESTER 2   /8
                   _____
                    Total

_____
THE LAUGH MASTER

Check out our

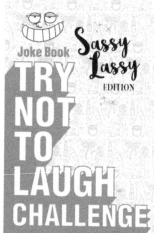

Visit our Amazon Store at:

other joke books!

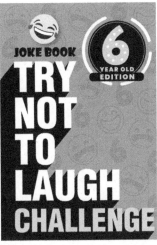

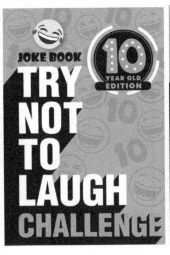
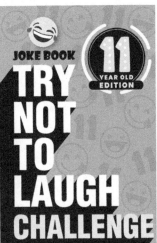
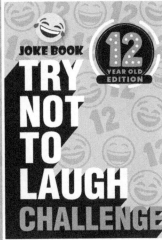